First World War
and Army of Occupation
War Diary
France, Belgium and Germany

46 DIVISION
Headquarters, Branches and Services
Royal Army Ordnance Corps
Deputy Assistant Director Ordnance Services
1 March 1915 - 28 February 1919

WO95/2672/2

The Naval & Military Press Ltd
www.nmarchive.com
Published in association with The National Archives

Published by

The Naval & Military Press Ltd

Unit 10 Ridgewood Industrial Park,

Uckfield, East Sussex,

TN22 5QE England

Tel: +44 (0) 1825 749494

www.naval-military-press.com

www.nmarchive.com

This diary has been reprinted in facsimile from the original. Any imperfections are inevitably reproduced and the quality may fall short of modern type and cartographic standards.

© **Crown Copyright**
Images reproduced by permission of The National Archives, London, England, 2015.

Contents

Document type	Place/Title	Date From	Date To
Heading	WO95/2672/2 Deputy Assistant Director Ordnance Services		
Heading	DADOS. 1st North Midland Divn Vol I		
War Diary		01/03/1915	30/03/1915
Heading	DADOS. 46th Division Vol II 6-13.4.15		
War Diary		06/04/1915	13/04/1915
Heading	DADOS. 46th (NM) Division Vol III May 1915		
War Diary		00/05/1915	00/05/1915
Heading	46th Division. DADOS. 46th Division. Vol IV		
War Diary		23/06/1915	23/06/1915
Heading	46th Division. DADOS. 46th Division Vol V		
Heading	War Diary of D.A.D.O.S. 46th Division (Major R.H. Kelly) From 1.4.15 To 31.7.1		
War Diary		15/07/1915	23/07/1915
Heading	46th Division DADOS. 46th Divn Vol Vi August 1.15		
Heading	War Diary of D.A.O. OF 46th Division (Major Kelly And) From 1.8.15 To 31.8.15		
War Diary		00/08/1915	00/08/1915
War Diary	Reference Map Sheet 28 9.7.d. Near Poperinghe	31/08/1915	31/08/1915
Heading	46th Division. D.A.D.O.S. 46th Division Vol VII Sept. 15		
Heading	War Diary of D.A.D.O.S. 46th Divn. (Major Kelly a.o.D) From 1-9-15 To 30-9-15		
War Diary		00/09/1915	29/09/1915
Heading	46th Division. D.A.D.O.S. 46th L (N.M) Div Oct 15 Vol VIII		
Miscellaneous	D A G 3rd Echelon G.H.Q War Diary Base	11/11/1915	11/11/1915
Miscellaneous	Confidential		
War Diary		02/10/1915	31/10/1915
War Diary	Bethune	31/10/1915	31/10/1915
Heading	DADOS 46th Div. Nov 1915 Vol IX		
War Diary		01/11/1915	30/11/1915
Heading	War Diary Major W.W. Blades DADOS 46 Division. From 1.12.15 to 31.12.15		
War Diary	Lagorgue	01/12/1915	02/12/1915
War Diary	Meville	03/12/1915	18/12/1915
War Diary	La Lacque	20/12/1915	31/12/1915
Heading	War Diary of Major W.W. Blades D.A.D.O.S. 46th Division Vol XI		
War Diary	La Lacque	01/01/1916	10/01/1916
War Diary	Marseilles	11/01/1916	27/01/1916
War Diary	Pontremy	27/01/1916	27/01/1916
Heading	War Diary of Major W.W. Blades D.A.D.O.S. 46 Division From 1st February. 1916. To 29th. February. 1916. Vol XII W.W. Blades. Major. D.A.D.O.S. 46 Division		
War Diary	Pont Remy	01/02/1916	19/02/1916
War Diary	Ribeaucourt	19/02/1916	29/02/1916
War Diary	In The Field	01/08/1916	31/08/1916
Miscellaneous	Herewith War Diary of D.A.D.O.S.	02/12/1916	02/12/1916

War Diary	Bavincourt	01/09/1916	31/10/1916
War Diary	Frohen-Le-Grand.	01/11/1916	02/11/1916
War Diary	St Riquier 4th.	03/11/1916	22/11/1916
War Diary	Frohen-Le-Grand.	23/11/1916	30/11/1916
War Diary	Lucheux	25/11/1916	06/12/1916
War Diary	Henu	07/12/1916	20/03/1917
War Diary	Couin	21/03/1917	23/03/1917
War Diary	Villers	24/03/1917	24/03/1917
War Diary	Bocage	25/03/1917	25/03/1917
War Diary	Dury	26/03/1917	26/03/1917
War Diary	In Car	27/03/1917	27/03/1917
War Diary	Lillers	28/03/1917	28/03/1917
War Diary	Fontes	29/03/1917	13/04/1917
War Diary	Busnes	14/04/1917	16/04/1917
War Diary	Lebeuvriere	17/04/1917	19/04/1917
War Diary	Sains	20/04/1917	15/05/1917
War Diary	Sains-En-Gohelle	16/05/1917	14/07/1917
War Diary	Ourton	15/07/1917	28/07/1917
War Diary	Labourse	29/07/1917	26/12/1917
War Diary	Busnes	27/12/1917	31/12/1917
War Diary	Labourse	01/01/1918	20/01/1918
War Diary	Busnes	21/01/1918	08/02/1918
War Diary	Bomy	09/02/1918	02/03/1918
War Diary	Fouquieres	03/03/1918	28/03/1918
War Diary	Bracquemont	29/03/1918	12/04/1918
War Diary	Bruay	13/04/1918	24/04/1918
War Diary	Gosnay	25/04/1918	11/09/1918
War Diary	Beaucourt	12/09/1918	19/09/1918
War Diary	Estrees	19/09/1918	08/10/1918
War Diary	Vendelles	09/10/1918	19/10/1918
War Diary	Fresnoy	29/10/1918	06/11/1918
War Diary	Catillon	07/11/1918	12/11/1918
War Diary	Sains Du Nord	13/11/1918	15/11/1918
War Diary	Landrecies	16/11/1918	09/01/1919
War Diary	Le Cateau	10/01/1919	31/01/1919
Miscellaneous	46th. Division. No. W.D.2	30/03/1919	30/03/1919
War Diary	Le Cateau.	01/02/1919	28/02/1919

WO95/2672/2
Deputy Assistant Director
Ordnance Services

131/4885

DCoS

DADOS. 1st North Midland Divn

Vol I. 1 – Sept 3.15
       30

WAR DIARY
or
INTELLIGENCE SUMMARY.
(Erase heading not required.)

1/1st N. Midland Divn T.F. D.A.D.O.S.

Army Form C. 2118.

Instructions regarding War Diaries and Intelligence Summaries are contained in F.S. Regs., Part II. and the Staff Manual respectively. Title pages will be prepared in manuscript.

Hour, Date, Place	Summary of Events and Information	Remarks and references to Appendices
1915	1/1st North Midland Division.	
1st March	D.A.D.O.S.	
	Divl Hd Qrs entrained at HAVRE to proceed to the front.	
2nd "	Arrived at CASSEL station and remained in billets at OXELEARE for a week. As the Division was equipped before leaving England there was not much to do as regards A.O.D. Services on first arrival. It was not till after arrival at MERRIS that any considerable demands were made by units.	
6 "	On arrival at HAVRE the Division was supplied with warm under-clothing, fur waistcoats etc, and it was found	

WAR DIARY
or
INTELLIGENCE SUMMARY
(Erase heading not required.)

D.A.D.O.S. N. Midland Divn T.F.   Army Form C. 2118.

Hour, Date, Place	Summary of Events and Information	Remarks and references to Appendices
30th March	found at once that the men did not require this warm clothing, and some difficulty was experienced in carrying it. Arrangements were however made to withdraw all the warm clothing from the whole force. The Division withdrew all woollen clothing and stored it at CAESTRE which was then rail head. Instructions were then received regarding the railway arrangements for carrying these articles to PARIS for cleaning and overhaul and on 30/3 three truck loads were despatched. Owing to frequent moves and the rather wide area covered by the Division it was not possible to eke more than distribute at once the stores received. Railhead was five miles from Div H.Q. and many units were eight miles from rail head which made it impossible to have a central place to collect stores for distribution. Consequently stores were distributed direct from Rail head. This method was a difficult one and very extravagant.	

R.W. Kelly Major in
D.A.D.O.S. N. Mid. Divn

121/5314.

DADOS. 46th Division

Vol II 6-13.4.15

WAR DIARY
or
INTELLIGENCE SUMMARY.
(Erase heading not required.)

Army Form C. 2118.

Hour, Date, Place	Summary of Events and Information	Remarks and references to Appendices
1915 6th April	1/1st North Midland Division D.A.D.O.S. Division took over trenches from 5th Div'n and Headquarters moved to ST JAN CAPEL. The Ordnance Store – or rather DUMP – was not the town used in this country was placed in BAILLIEUL – This was the most suitable and convenient place being close to Railhead and a centre for roads leading to the positions of the various units. As soon as huts – hot over benches and settled huts – camp & billets large demands were made on A.O.D. for	

WAR DIARY
INTELLIGENCE SUMMARY.
(Erase heading not required.)

Army Form C. 2118.

Instructions regarding War Diaries and Intelligence Summaries are contained in F. S. Regs., Part II. and the Staff Manual respectively. Title pages will be prepared in manuscript.

Hour, Date, Place	Summary of Events and Information	Remarks and references to Appendices
13 April	2 A.O.S. 1st N. M. Dn. — For stores both in replacement [?] and for special stores for trenches — a large demand was made for stores for use in connection with countermines and for special stores, periscopes, very lights &c. The whole month was passed in the ordinary routine of demanding & issuing stores — On the whole the supply from Base was brought and is satisfactory and there is nothing to call for special mention. On the night of the 12/13 a Zeppelin	II

WAR DIARY
INTELLIGENCE SUMMARY.
(Erase heading not required.)

Army Form C. 2118.

Hour, Date, Place	Summary of Events and Information	Remarks and references to Appendices
April 13	2.A.O.S. 1/1st N. M. Division. 2 Zeppelin airship came over the town about 11 p.m. and dropped explosive not incendiary bombs on the town. Two bombs dropped on a house 30 yds from the building occupied by the R.P. Set. 6 horses were killed and 2 serious slaves back weighing about 30 lb were thrown up and fell through the roof into the top room where some of the men were sleeping - no one was injured - the building is a 4 story building on the force of the explosion was very great - nothing of home was blown up - the whole family killed. R.W. Wally Major in D.A.D.O.S. 1/1/N. M. Div	

121/5536

D.D.O.S.

D.A.D.O.S. 46th (NM) Division.

Vol III — May 1915.

Army Form C. 2118.

WAR DIARY
or
~~INTELLIGENCE~~ SUMMARY.
(Erase heading not required.)

Instructions regarding War Diaries and Intelligence Summaries are contained in F.S. Regs., Part II. and the Staff Manual respectively. Title pages will be prepared in manuscript.

Hour, Date, Place	Summary of Events and Information	Remarks and references to Appendices
1915 May	War diary. D.A.D.O.S. 46th (North Midland) Division. The division did not move during the month and consequently there is nothing to record beyond the daily routine of supply of stores. The title of the Division was altered and it was given a number — the 46th — the words "North Midland" being added in brackets as shown at head of this sheet. During the month the Germans began the use of asphyxiating gas and a call was made for T.P. Box respirators. At first all suitable material that was available locally was bought up and made up into respirators, but in a few days supplies came from England, and a regular issue of respirators was made to troops. The first issue was made	

Army Form C. 2118.

WAR DIARY
or
INTELLIGENCE SUMMARY. 2nd Sheet
(Erase heading not required.)

Hour, Date, Place	Summary of Events and Information	Remarks and references to Appendices
May 1915	made only to men actually in the firing line but later it was found that the case of apparently far more men didn't arise was made to all officers & men - Later on a supply of flannel "wrote bands" with celluloid eyepieces was authorised for all officers & men except A.S.C. and A.V.C. Up to the end of the month these had not been received. A complaint was received from 10 BN Bde that rifles jammed at rapid fire. A second trial was made under general supervision & it was found that always rifles of the Diss own did not jam. But it also × chair ammunition that were fired (from a/l/same) is the type one ×— a cramped or strained position was owing to fired and difficulty in reloading was owing to the	×

RW Wilson Lieut Col OC 46 Bgn

rifles.

181/6065

46th Division

DADOS. 46th Division

Vol IV

Army Form C. 2118.

WAR DIARY
or
~~INTELLIGENCE SUMMARY~~
(Erase heading not required.)

Instructions regarding War Diaries and Intelligence Summaries are contained in F.S. Regs., Part II. and the Staff Manual respectively. Title pages will be prepared in manuscript.

Hour, Date, Place	Summary of Events and Information	Remarks and references to Appendices
1915 June	~~War Diary~~ 46th (North Midland) Division D.A.D.O.S. The supply of Smoke helmets which were intended to replace the ~~cod~~ anti-gas respirators came to hand slowly. Otherwise ordinary routine duties occupied the month until the Division was ordered to move to an area near POPERINGHE to take over ground from the 50th while the 50th moved down and took over the ground we held.	
23-6-15	The dump and Mice were moved	

Army Form C. 2118.

WAR DIARY
~~INTELLIGENCE SUMMARY.~~
(Erase heading not required.)

Instructions regarding War Diaries and Intelligence Summaries are contained in F. S. Regs., Part II. and the Staff Manual respectively. Title pages will be prepared in manuscript.

Hour, Date, Place	Summary of Events and Information	Remarks and references to Appendices
1915 June 23	D.A.D.S. 46th (North Midland) Division moves to OUDERDOM. The head had war CAESTRE. No other event occurred that calls for any notice. W.W. Kelly Major D.A.D.S. 46th (North Midland) Division	

121/6390

46th Division

DADOS. 46th Division

Vol V

July 1915

Army Form C. 2118.

WAR DIARY
INTELLIGENCE SUMMARY.
(Erase heading not required.)

Hour, Date, Place	Summary of Events and Information	Remarks and references to Appendices
	Confidential. War Diary of D.A.D.O.S. 46th Division. (Major R.W. Kelly) a.d. From: 1. 7. 15. To 31. 7. 15.	

Instructions regarding War Diaries and Intelligence Summaries are contained in F. S. Regs., Part II. and the Staff Manual respectively. Title pages will be prepared in manuscript.

WAR DIARY
~~INTELLIGENCE~~ SUMMARY
(Erase heading not required.)

Army Form C. 2118.

July 1915

Hour, Date, Place	Summary of Events and Information	Remarks and references to Appendices
15th July.	46th (North Midland) Division D.A.D.O.S. Railhead was changed to BAILLIEUL. No events beyond ordinary routine took place during early portion of the month. Demands from units were rather below the average and ordinary routine work was not heavy.	
23rd July.	Instructions were received to change areas with the 3rd Division and arrangements were accordingly made with the D.A.D.O.S. but on 23rd the enemy shelled OUDERDOM and put 4 shell within 150 yds of the building used as store. The store was quiet at a road junction and no doubt it was the road junction that was the objective. The dump was therefore moved to the position	

WAR DIARY
INTELLIGENCE SUMMARY.

(Erase heading not required.)

Army Form C. 2118.

July 1915

Hour, Date, Place	Summary of Events and Information	Remarks and references to Appendices
23 July	Position occupied by the 11th Division H.Q.s and he moved later to a farm. He did not move into the building I had vacated. The arrangements for the winter campaign begun to come up for consideration. A plan for hutments was drawn up. The roads and approaches to dumps were improved. For gunpower I was making bricks were obtained from ruined houses in YPRES. Such removal of material was under the strict supervision of the Belgian authorities and the A.P.M.	R W Kelly Captain DAAQMG 46th Divn

121/6734

46th Division

DADOS. 46th Divn

Vol VI
August 15

Army Form C. 2118.

WAR DIARY
INTELLIGENCE SUMMARY.
(Erase heading not required.)

Confidential

War Diary of
D.A.D.S.
46th Division
(Major Kelly. ADS)

From :- 1. 8. 15.
To :- 31. 8. 15.

Stamp: A.G.3 OFFICE AT THE BASE, 19 SEP. 1915, A.O.C. SECTION

WAR DIARY
INTELLIGENCE SUMMARY.
(Erase heading not required.)

Army Form C. 2118.

Hour, Date, Place	Summary of Events and Information	Remarks and references to Appendices
August 1915	46th (North Midland) Division D.A.D.O.S. No change took place during the month as regards the situation of the dumps. Owing to the accommodation in the barn used as store being insufficient, tarpaulins were put up to cover over of the stores while being laid out for issue. The question of winter quartering and supply of ammunition of the winter stores —	

Army Form C. 2118.

WAR DIARY
INTELLIGENCE SUMMARY.
(Erase heading not required.)

August 1915

Hour, Date, Place	Summary of Events and Information	Remarks and references to Appendices
Aug 1915	There is nothing special to record regarding the recent ammune & stores — the ordinary routine work of the detachment was carried on without interruption. The instruction in a new pattern of smoke helmet — the Tube pattern, compared with the "P" solution — has gone forwards the end of the month. Issues to the undermentioned & this pattern were completed by the 31st. The old pattern helmet which has been used was now —	

Army Form C. 2118.

WAR DIARY
or
INTELLIGENCE SUMMARY.
(Erase heading not required.)

August 1915

Instructions regarding War Diaries and Intelligence
Summaries are contained in F. S. Regs., Part II.
and the Staff Manual respectively. Title pages
will be prepared in manuscript.

Hour, Date, Place	Summary of Events and Information	Remarks and references to Appendices
Bivouac Mot-djuit 28 Near POPERINGHE. 31/8/15	party withdrawn and every man of RA RE Infantry, RAMC had to have one tube pattern and one film eye-piece pattern helmet in possession. Orders instructions were thus suspended but no instructions were received regarding their disposal — [signature] Capt'n 2/A Coy 46 (N. M.) Div	

Forms/C. 2118/10

46th Division

12/7049

D.A.D.O.S 46th Division

Vol VII

Sept. 15

Army Form C. 2118.

WAR DIARY
or
INTELLIGENCE SUMMARY.
(Erase heading not required.)

Confidential

War Diary of :-
D.A.D.O.S. 46th Div.
(Major Kelly. A.O.D.)

From :- 1-9-15.
To :- 30-9-15.

7-OCT 1915

Army Form C. 2118.

WAR DIARY
or
INTELLIGENCE SUMMARY.
(Erase heading not required.)

Hour, Date, Place	Summary of Events and Information	Remarks and references to Appendices
September 1915	D.A.D.O.S. 46th (North Midland) Division. The question of issue of winter clothing was considered. Issue of no blanket per man was authorised and made. Issue of tents began. 240 were allotted to the Division and issue made to units allotted by Div. Commander. Two 15 P.R B.L. guns were condemned by I.O.M. leaving necessit. the limbs of these guns ongoing, these were the first case of a 15 P.R gun becoming	

WAR DIARY or INTELLIGENCE SUMMARY

Army Form C. 2118.

Hour, Date, Place	Summary of Events and Information	Remarks and references to Appendices
Sept 1915	Weather unseasonable since arrival in the country seven months before. The sun has all had a good deal of firing to do, and has looked very well. Apart from ordinary routine work there was nothing to record.	
29 N Sept	Until orders were suddenly received to leave the YPRES salient and the II Army and proceed to BETHUNE to join the Ist not Army which was then engaged in making a big attack on the German trenches	[signature] M.S. Wally Major RFA Cmdg 46th Bn

121/7496

46th Division

A.A. & Q.M.G. 46th (N.M.) Divn

Dec 15

Vol VIII

ON HIS MAJESTY'S SERVICE.

DAG 3rd Echelon GHQ
Base

11 NOV 1915

Confidential

Army Form C. 2118.

WAR DIARY
or
INTELLIGENCE SUMMARY.
(Erase heading not required.)

Instructions regarding War Diaries and Intelligence Summaries are contained in F.S. Regs., Part II. and the Staff Manual respectively. Title pages will be prepared in manuscript.

Hour, Date, Place	Summary of Events and Information	Remarks and references to Appendices
2nd Oct 1915	He moves to Bethune began. There was great difficulty in finding any building to use as dump, and billets were also very hard to find owing to the large number of troops in the area, and the fact that all large stores had been appropriated by the various Ambulances for use of wounded. Eventually at 5.30 am Dump was formed at 47 Rue D'Aire. Some units were near enough to come in and draw stores direct, but the majority to the units were supplied by convoy.	

Army Form C. 2118.

WAR DIARY
or
INTELLIGENCE SUMMARY.
(Erase heading not required.)

Instructions regarding War Diaries and Intelligence Summaries are contained in F.S. Regs., Part II. and the Staff Manual respectively. Title pages will be prepared in manuscript.

Hour, Date, Place	Summary of Events and Information	Remarks and references to Appendices
5th Oct.	Information was given me that the Division was shortly to take part in a big attack on the German at Hohenzollern Redoubt and Fosse 8 — Consequently certain plans, one being bomb carriers, were urgently required and considerable mounting. It was found that the facilities for local purchase were much greater here than in the 3rd Army area, which was a great assistance. A number of articles such as Vermorel Sprayers, Solum breathing sets (for use of machine gunners during gas attack), steel helmets, were sent by the Division for use during the attack — G.O.C. moves to Div. advance

12/10/15

Army Form C. 2118.

WAR DIARY
or
INTELLIGENCE SUMMARY.
(Erase heading not required.)

Hour, Date, Place	Summary of Events and Information	Remarks and references to Appendices
12/10/15	Advanced Hd Qrs. as the above but by Motor Divisions left coming in up to the last minute they had to cut up to the furthest possible point — this was VERMELLES where the most advanced dumps of RE stores had been formed — these dumps were in the vaults of a brewery and the cellars of the houses.	
13/10/15	The attack was timed for 2 p.m. all traffic was to cease at 11-30 a.m. and the last Lewis (machine) sets were only delivered by motor car just at 11 am. The attack resulted in the capture only portion of the objective and the British continued about 3000 casualties. A lot of equipment of all kinds was	

WAR DIARY
or
INTELLIGENCE SUMMARY.
(Erase heading not required.)

Army Form C. 2118.

Instructions regarding War Diaries and Intelligence Summaries are contained in F.S. Regs., Part II. and the Staff Manual respectively. Title pages will be prepared in manuscript.

Hour, Date, Place	Summary of Events and Information	Remarks and references to Appendices
13/10/15	lost in the attack and the next week was a busy one getting lost & damaged articles replaced. The greatest difficulty was to get units to own in lists of their requirements — all demands were promptly met by the Base.	
19/10/15	The Town Major's orders me to move my Office & stores to another party of the town but I was outside XI Corps area. So I moved to 51 Boulevarde DesGeorges near the railway station.	
31/10/15	Orders were received that the Divisions were to move to LESTREM, to relieve the LAHORE Division. The XI Corps was relieving the Indian Corps, which was being taken up and was leaving France — the XI Corps consisted of B	

Army Form C. 2118.

WAR DIARY
or
INTELLIGENCE SUMMARY.
(Erase heading not required.)

Hour, Date, Place	Summary of Events and Information	Remarks and references to Appendices
31/10/15 BETHUNE	consisted of Guards 46th and 12th Division. The 12th Division left the corps and the 19th infantry replaced it. The heaviest work during the month was the issue of winter clothing. J.R.W Harris Major 46th Div 4/11/15	

121/7637

Vol IX

WAR DIARY
or
INTELLIGENCE SUMMARY.
(Erase heading not required.)

Army Form C. 2118.

D.A.D.O.S.

46th (North Midland) Division.

Hour, Date, Place	Summary of Events and Information	Remarks and references to Appendices
1/11/15	Proceeded to LAHORE. On arrival took over billets. Great difficulty experienced in getting any place. Decided to go to MERVILLE entire, a few Mice & little else were shut on insufficient store.	
2/4 & 5	Division moved by detachments to new area. As LAHORE Div' Ordnance had not moved I could not move to MERVILLE.	
6th	As store at BETHUNE was required by Corps Major J. Munroe office & store to MERVILLE and carried on in in a shed & in a marquee tent till the Lahore Division Ordnance moved out.	

Army Form C. 2118.

WAR DIARY
or
~~INTELLIGENCE SUMMARY.~~
(Erase heading not required.)

Instructions regarding War Diaries and Intelligence Summaries are contained in F.S. Regs., Part II. and the Staff Manual respectively. Title pages will be prepared in manuscript.

Hour, Date, Place	Summary of Events and Information	Remarks and references to Appendices
November 1915 21st.-	Railhead moved from BETHUNE. The principal duty during month was the issue of winter clothing. This was not quite completed by end of month, the chief difficulty being to obtain Vests Woollen. A complaint was received from the 13th Infantry Brigade that the oil supplied for rifles was liable to freeze and came fifty to zero. I went to Bd H? Qrs to investigate all but could not arrive at any conclusion, the Sr Ord has no answer in attendance nor has the question been referred to any	

WAR DIARY
~~INTELLIGENCE SUMMARY~~

Army Form C. 2118.

(Erase heading not required.)

Hour, Date, Place	Summary of Events and Information	Remarks and references to Appendices
November 1915	To any of the armourers in the B.E. — I made experiments myself and found that the oil did not freeze and that rifles certainly worked slightly stiffly but would fire — the matter was still under observation at end of month. No complaints were made by any other units.	

30/11/15

R.M. Kelly
Armourer
A.D.O.S. 46th Divn

War Diary

Major W.W. Blades.

D.A.D.O.S. 46' Division.

From 1.12.15
to 31.12.15

W.W. Blades. Major.
D.A.D.O.S. 46' Division.

Vol X

WAR DIARY
INTELLIGENCE SUMMARY

(Erase heading not required.)

Army Form C. 2118

Place	Date	Hour	Summary of Events and Information	Remarks and references to Appendices
LA GORGUE	1/12/15		Received weekly consignment of boots today. Borris quickly loaded & despatched at midday. Also I instructed me to demand four hundred converted trench mortars. A wire for these was accordingly sent to the Base. A.P.M. instructed that five Runners coming in from battalion for the signallers of the 1st. & 2nd. Guards Brigade be purchased, and a call made as to their suitability. A number of lorries were received from 2 Cavalry Brigade Staff and issued to the 1st. & 3rd. Guards Brigades. The three representatives from the machine gun companies came in to pick up their indents for stores according to the new manual, store called. They took their indents away and promised to return them in the morning.	
	2/12/15		Purchased from M. Rennie, Merville, 20 suits of dungaree clothing for use of fatigue parties working on the coal barges. Received another indent from O/75 Lol. R.F.A. for boots, the number of which used by this battery is most excessive. I arranged with the Adjutant to go down to see the O.C. O/75 or	

Army Form C. 2118

WAR DIARY
INTELLIGENCE SUMMARY
(Erase heading not required.)

Instructions regarding War Diaries and Intelligence Summaries are contained in F. S. Regs., Part II. and the Staff Manual respectively. Title Pages will be prepared in manuscript.

Place	Date	Hour	Summary of Events and Information	Remarks and references to Appendices
LACORGUE	2/12/15		D.A.Q.M.G. enquired for stands for rifle grenades. On reference to B.O.O. he instructed me to go to A.O.D. workshop at [?], Hazebrouck where these stands were first made. Will go tomorrow.	wish
MERVILLE	3/12/15		Received instructions from B.O.O. 1st Army to take over duties of B.O.O. He Bruneau in exchange with Major Kelly. The exchange was completed and duly reported at each point. Hd. Qrs. Went to Aire to see B.O.O. 2nd with reference to early move of 46th Division and received the necessary instructions.	
	4/12/15		Received instructions from B.O.O. as to stores to be withdrawn from [?] but very much doubt if it is than that all must be demand [?] [?] Truly	want
	5/12		Went to Point Hd. Qrs. and arranged which A.Q.M.G. for a circular to be sent to Units instructing them what action to take with reference to return of stores not obtained by Indent. Store Dates. Received instructions from B.D.O. 1st Army, that each man was to take two blankets but to return fur waistcoats, leather [?], fingerless gloves & mackintosh capes. Informed A.Q.M.G. and	want

WAR DIARY
—or—
INTELLIGENCE SUMMARY.
(Erase heading not required.)

Army Form C. 2118.

64

Hour, Date, Place	Summary of Events and Information	Remarks and references to Appendices
MERVILLE		
5/12/15	and had circular to units amended accordingly. Called in at Mill, Calonne, and instructed the N.C.O. that units who had returned [?] would draw them again as soon as possible.	hours
6/12/15	Went to Divl. Hd. Qrs. this morning. Told A.Q.M.G. I would visit all Bdes. Hd. Qrs. as early as possible. Visited 139. Inf. Bde. Hd. Qrs. and brought to notice of Staff Captain two cases of returns demands for clothing. Staff Captain stated he had not received units indented for. On looking into the matter I find his indent was received too late for such issue. Was sent for at 6pm. to see the E.O.C. who marched into the general condition	

WAR DIARY
INTELLIGENCE SUMMARY.
(Erase heading not required.)

Army Form C. 2118.

Hour, Date, Place	Summary of Events and Information	Remarks and references to Appendices
MERVILLE 6/12/15.		
4/12/15.	Condition of Ordnance Supply. I assured him that it was on satisfactory experience under the circumstances. I went to office of C.R.O., 46' Division, but could only find the A/D.C. I explained to that officer what underclothing should be in possession of each man & the steps to be taken for its exchange at the Corps Laundry. Visited 1/1, 1/2, & 2/1 N. Midland Fd. Cos. Representatives of each unit complained of non-issue of sizes 9 & 4, 10's in boots. On return to office I find that with the exception of 9's due to 1/2 Fd Co. last week all boots indented for have been duly supplied, and signature held. 9 & 9's not waited last week [man] ready to be drawn. G.O.C. Comdg. 137 Inf. Bde, called at the	ways.
	during my absence and complained that ...	

WAR DIARY
INTELLIGENCE SUMMARY
(Erase heading not required.)

Army Form C. 2118.

Instructions regarding War Diaries and Intelligence Summaries are contained in F.S. Regs., Part II. and the Staff Manual respectively. Title pages will be prepared in manuscript.

6/

Hour, Date, Place	Summary of Events and Information	Remarks and references to Appendices
MERVILLE. 7.6.15	complained that his boots/coats could not get what they indexed for. Immediately after he left, from incidents from battalions in the Brigade were received for enormous quantities of equipment &c. I went out to endeavour to find the Std. Bn. of this Brigade but failed.	own
8.6.15	Saw the Adj. commdg. 137th. Inf. Bde. and showed him several incidents from his brigade for new large quantities of web equipment. The O.C. took notes of various items with a view to further action. G.O.C. Division visited the Office. He was shown several incidents from the 137th Bde., which made it perfectly clean that great care was necessary in the care of equipment and clothing	words

Army Form C. 2118.

WAR DIARY
or
INTELLIGENCE SUMMARY.
(Erase heading not required.)

Hour, Date, Place	Summary of Events and Information	Remarks and references to Appendices
MERVILLE 8.12.15	D.A.Q. 1st. Army visited the office. The question of the return of equipment by the Division was discussed.	wire
9.12.15	Ranged Halsey Car for a sunbeam from French Supply Column. Went to Bethune to try to purchase from supplier for brushing clothing, but could find nothing suitable. Received instructions from Divnl. Hd. Qrs. to attend a conference at 11 a.m. tomorrow, on the subject of Clothing & equipment.	wire
10.12.15	Attended a conference at Divnl. Hd. Qrs. on the subject of excessive issues of Clothing & equipment to units of the Division, & O.C. directed that no extra issues to be viewed unless the irrecoverable one.	reply

Forms/C. 2118/10

WAR DIARY
INTELLIGENCE SUMMARY
(Erase heading not required.)

Army Form C. 2118.

Hour, Date, Place	Summary of Events and Information	Remarks and references to Appendices
MERVILLE 10/9/15	He was produced, and all concurred to be paid for. Lt. Condr. Hendy obtained a medical certificate that he was unfit to accompany the Division, so I wired B.S.os 1st Army asking that an exchange might be effected between he and Lt. Condr. Bougard, provided S.os, Guards Division soon agreed.	
11/9/15	Large consignment of Jerseys, Knives, Shirts, Pantaloons, etc. received, which nearly meet all drain out. Purchase 120 pounds Khaki for clothing. There will be rivited equally to the 128 & 129 Brigades. Received instructions from B.S.os 1st Army to translate Lt. Condr. Hendy to Guards Divn. Bougard in exchange with the condr. Bougard....	

WAR DIARY
INTELLIGENCE SUMMARY.
(Erase heading not required.)

Army Form C. 2118.

Instructions regarding War Diaries and Intelligence Summaries are contained in F.S. Regs., Part II. and the Staff Manual respectively. Title pages will be prepared in manuscript.

Hour, Date, Place	Summary of Events and Information	Remarks and references to Appendices
MERVILLE 12/12/15	Divisional Rearguard joined from Guards Division and Lieut. Constructor S. Heady transferred thereto. Lists of stores issued by units to be still outstanding to them several very discrepancies when compared with A.D. ascertaining incidents. This is not to be wondered at.	
13/12/15	Princ. Vet. Sn. Ransomed all small horse and mule shoes. A wire was sent to Corps accordingly. B.G. Q.M.G. instructed me that R.E. Horses are attached men from 5th North Staffs. Regt. might be returned when the Division moves. D.A.O.S. 1st Army wired that it is arranged to replace the winter S.D. Caps already..	

WAR DIARY
INTELLIGENCE SUMMARY.
(Erase heading not required.)

Army Form C. 2118.

Hour, Date, Place	Summary of Events and Information	Remarks and references to Appendices
MERVILLE 13/2/15	Supplied. The car was sent to Supply Column for repairs. Very inconvenient not being able to get about to units. The Res. men paid today.	
14/2/15	Received intimation from Bdos. 1st. Army that 4 "5" Howitzers had arrived at Hinnie & would be sent up as soon as a march could be obtained. Went to 6th. Sherwood Foresters in hun Stores. Found a large quantity of clothing apparently surplus. The R. Am. was instructed that everything he did not want was to be put on rails for the Base at once. Many visitors today, whose sole object seemed to be to get more stores. e.g. I inquired why prophozning traps for use guns, tripods battle sights, re were wish.	wish. wish.

Army Form C. 2118.

WAR DIARY
or
INTELLIGENCE SUMMARY.
(Erase heading not required.)

Hour, Date, Place	Summary of Events and Information	Remarks and references to Appendices
MERVILLE 14.12.15	were being withdrawn, so I quoted the 1st. Army Orders and stated that I had again tried & received instructions confirming the instructions already given.	wire.
15.12.15	Spoke to A.Q.M.G. about the new arrangement for the Remitgen Rolls who was informed that the R.O.A. moved along deal with the stores. I went to see O.C. 1 Staff Battery, R.O.A. about ammunition saddlery, what was produced for my inspection, was quite unserviceable. Previewed more of Q.O. and was instructed by A.Q.M.G. that it would be better to accompany the supply Column, on we have stores to take with us.	
16.12.15	4.5 inch Hewitzer arrived this morning and were duly offloaded by the outlying Party, men have been found to be missing	wire.

morning wire. |

WAR DIARY or INTELLIGENCE SUMMARY

Army Form C. 2118.

(Erase heading not required.)

Hour, Date, Place	Summary of Events and Information	Remarks and references to Appendices
NERVILLE 10/11/15	and from the statement of the convoy men it would appear to have dropped off the train before reaching Allerville. A wire was received from D.A.D.R.Y. Allerville notifying the loss. In reply I informed that the cart when found, be sent on by the quickest possible route, to wire me immediately it were found. Major Jones from 1st Army, visited the depôt to see how the British stores were being returned. It was found that 24 Ammunition wagons have been received with the 4.5 inch equipment, and this morning eight G.S. wagons arrived with the Base Army Column. By this morning the men ordered to be transferred to B.a.c. to complete establishment, and eight men to the Base.	

WAR DIARY
INTELLIGENCE SUMMARY.
(Erase heading not required.)

Army Form C. 2118.

Instructions regarding War Diaries and Intelligence Summaries are contained in F.S. Regs., Part II. and the Staff Manual respectively. Title pages will be prepared in manuscript.

No 3

Hour, Date, Place	Summary of Events and Information	Remarks and references to Appendices
MERVILLE 14/2/15	Five truck loads of stores received today. This includes stores not received yesterday. Indents do not seem so numerous today. Major Lloyd Jones, R.A.M.C. called to discuss the question of issue of clothing to Field Ambulances. A.D.M.S. instructed me to recover the 19 telescopic sights returned by units and which, not bearing the W.D. mark, are the private property of battalions. In view of the large number of binoculars due to the Division, I invited attention of H.Q. R.A. of Brigades to the matter, or perhaps, they might like to raise instructions as to care of these articles in the future. 86 binoculars were stated by Base to be still due, and not available, nor wrips [?].	

WAR DIARY
INTELLIGENCE SUMMARY.
(Erase heading not required.)

Army Form C. 2118.

Hour, Date, Place	Summary of Events and Information	Remarks and references to Appendices
MERVILLE. 18.12.15	A.Q.M.G. 46'Divn. informed me that the Division moves on 19th inst. to an area behind the present one. Received a rather offensive letter from O.C. 5' Leicester Regt. in reply to a memo asking for information as to why certain surplus clothing was returned to railhead. This was handed to A.Q.M.G. A.Q.M.G. 11th Corps sent for me and asked as to number of magnifying sights and rifles with telescope sights.	mins.
19.12.15	Went to Ra Becau to arrange a new billet. Found a good barn there. A.Q.M.G. 11th Corps came to office re retreat for information in state of equipment of 46th Division. Such an area available was given him.	mins.

WAR DIARY or INTELLIGENCE SUMMARY

Army Form C. 2118.

Hour, Date, Place	Summary of Events and Information	Remarks and references to Appendices
LA LACQUE 20/11/918	Moved to LALACQUE. Transport was not satisfactory, on return lorries applied for were not sent. The move from Lorris was very short of heat. This state of affairs never occurred with men in the Guards Division. This det. including the old transport officers, drew not off uniate the whole of time, an articles I ordered to be packed up were nothing, were still unpacked this morning. The two escepts the C.E.. do not mention the enemy manual. Called on Nel Ind 131st Inf. to de., was kept over half hour, went on to S. & Staff. Regt. now the OC., who was acting Bde Commander, so appeared to be well acquainted with what had been done in OOP. for his battalion, anxious of having no knowledge additional mules observes noted.	

WAR DIARY
INTELLIGENCE SUMMARY.
(Erase heading not required.)

Army Form C. 2118.

Instructions regarding War Diaries and Intelligence Summaries are contained in F. S. Regs., Part II. and the Staff Manual respectively. Title pages will be prepared in manuscript.

Hour, Date, Place	Summary of Events and Information	Remarks and references to Appendices
LA LACQUE 21/12/15	A.Q.M.G. instructed me that the second Armoured Train should be taken by A.S.D. and not by units, owing to small amounts of transport they have available. Two lorries had to be sent to Marseille for Armoured Trains. The removal of stores from Railhead a corresponding amount to units never delayed.	
22.12.15	Visited Hd. Qrs. 138th Infantry Bde., and discussed with the Brigadier the question of transport of packhorses. He was agreed that the mule companies refused motherups to help the animals in the wagons, until the Brigade animals at its destination. A great many teams drawn today, there seems to me finally to the wants of this provision.	contd. contd.

Army Form C. 2118.

WAR DIARY
INTELLIGENCE SUMMARY.
(Erase heading not required.)

Instructions regarding War Diaries and Intelligence Summaries are contained in F.S. Regs., Part II. and the Staff Manual respectively. Title pages will be prepared in manuscript.

Hour, Date, Place	Summary of Events and Information	Remarks and references to Appendices
LA LACQUE 23/12/15	Received an indent from 1/5 South Staff. Regt. for web equipment to replace leather articles brought up by drafts. Referred the question to D.D.O.S. 1st Army, who instructed me that there was no authority for the exchange, on W.O. Letter 54/Infantry/1302, dy. 13.5.15 stated there would be the two descriptions in use at the same time. Was instructed by A.Q.M.G. of impending departure of several units, so 9 mules to teams to send no more stores for them. Issued smoke helmets into lorries of the Supply Columns for transport to destination of Division.	nil.
24/12/15	Very little doing today, there being no trucks in, other than one with a linseed wagon for the Divnl. train.	nil.
25/12/15	No truck arrived today, being few units came, there being little to issue.	nil.

Army Form C. 2118.

WAR DIARY
INTELLIGENCE SUMMARY.
(Erase heading not required.)

Instructions regarding War Diaries and Intelligence Summaries are contained in F. S. Regs., Part II. and the Staff Manual respectively. Title pages will be prepared in manuscript.

Hour, Date, Place	Summary of Events and Information	Remarks and references to Appendices
LA LACQUE 26/12/15	A fair amount of Stores arrived today, amongst them being a large number of "Rammers, earth," for the 5th. Batt. Derby Regt., originally demanded when this unit was the Pioneer Battalion. The Monmouth Regt. now being the Pioneer Bn. having left this area with the 137" Bde., the Rammers were returned to Bases. Visited the four battalions of the 138th Bde. but could only see the O.C.'s of 4 Leicesters + 5" Lincolns. Nothing of importance was required, other than wood returning material.	
27 to 31/12/15	On leave.	wish.
		Wickslades. Major. D.A.Q.G. 46 Division

Forms/C. 2118/10

War Diary
of
Major W.W. Blades.
D.A.D.O.S. 46th. Division.
From 1st. January, 1916
To 31st. January, 1916

W.W. Blades. Major.
D.A.D.O.S. 46 Division

Vol XI

Army Form C. 2118.

WAR DIARY
INTELLIGENCE SUMMARY.
(Erase heading not required.)

Instructions regarding War Diaries and Intelligence Summaries are contained in F.S. Regs., Part II. and the Staff Manual respectively. Title pages will be prepared in manuscript.

Place	Hour, Date	Summary of Events and Information	Remarks and references to Appendices
LA LACQUE.	1-1-16. 2.1.16	Leave. Rejoined 10 p.m. Returned at Folkestone 1 night. Reported at Brinl. Hd. Qrs. Informed by A.A. & Q.M.G. that supply column and various other units would not accompany the Division. This decision raised the question of smoke helmets, &c., which the supply column was conveying for A.O.D. I wired that unit to hand over everything to O.C. Horse and also asked that officer to send similar numbers to me as ones. wyns.	
	3.1.16	Despatched 2/C.A. Ironside at 11.15 a.m. to Marseilles from Bethune. A.A. & Q.M.G. informed me that the 138 Bde Hd. Qrs, the 4 + 5 Lincoln Regts, the 2 N.M. Field Ambulance, the 3 Section Signal Co. would leave on Wednesday 5th inst. for Marseilles. Smoke varies from the Bde are to these units were concealed by mine. I decided to send 2/Cpl. B. Garland & Pte. A. Stubley by the same train to arrive of C.A. Ironside.	wyns.

Army Form C. 2118.

WAR DIARY
or
INTELLIGENCE SUMMARY.
(Erase heading not required.)

Instructions regarding War Diaries and Intelligence Summaries are contained in F.S. Regs., Part II. and the Staff Manual respectively. Title pages will be prepared in manuscript.

80

Hour, Date, Place	Summary of Events and Information	Remarks and references to Appendices
LALACQUE 3.1.16	The 2nd in. of the 5th Rats Beverley Regt. came today and produced a list of outstanding indents for towels, which he said he was unable to get at the 11th Div. Corps Roundup. Purchased 100. Received several indents from batteries of R.F.A. for excessive quantities of clothing. These were referred to C. or. R.F.A. who, I am glad to say, quite appreciates the matter. Does not approve of such waste.	nil.
4.1.16	Drew 500 francs from Field Cashier, with a view to purchase of such towels as may be wanted. Spoke with smoke helmets today. A.A. & Q.M.G. agreed that the letters from would be to raid them straight through to brewerises.	nil.

Army Form C. 2118.

WAR DIARY
or
INTELLIGENCE SUMMARY.
(Erase heading not required.)

8/

Instructions regarding War Diaries and Intelligence Summaries are contained in F.S. Regs., Part II. and the Staff Manual respectively. Title pages will be prepared in manuscript.

Hour, Date, Place	Summary of Events and Information	Remarks and references to Appendices
LA LACQUE. 4.1.16.	Received intimation from A.A. + Q.M.G. of further departures of units of this Division, so wired Boré to cease all issues on outstanding indents.	nil.
5.1.16	Two bushels of smoke helmets, gas goggles, and satchels, received from Boré this morning and recommended to O.C. Marseilles. Undercharge of Rifle Edwardes, Sub-condr. Bawley and two men joined 138th Infantry Batn. Hdrs. Rs. for duty on leaving the crew. Capt. Wilson, E.S. 46th Division, Marseilles, wired that 2/conclr. Wanter and one man were leaving on the 7th inst. with ammunition, and asked for another hovronic officer to be sent at once.	nil.

Forms/C. 2118/10

Army Form C. 2118

WAR DIARY
INTELLIGENCE SUMMARY
(Erase heading not required.)

Place	Date	Hour	Summary of Events and Information	Remarks and references to Appendices
LA LACQUE	6/1/16		Called at 1st Army Hd. Qrs. to explain to D.D.O.S. the present position of Ordnance Stores in the Division. Asked A.Q. & Q.M.G. what decision had been arrived at as to the spare parts for 18 pr. guns and 4.5" howitzers, carried by the Divnl. Amn. Col.; but was informed that no further instructions had been received. Went to office of D.D.O.S. 1st Army, drove this important question & Major Jones promised to 'phone for information & let me know result tomorrow. Sew. B. Neilson + P.te. Irving, joined Hd. Qrs. 139th Inf. Bde. and left this area. Brought to notice of A.A. & Q.M.G. the practice of some batteries of hiring in mobile carts daily. Received instructions from A.A. & Q.M.G. to move with Divnl. Hd. Qrs. on 9th inst.	Initials.
			D.D.O.S. 1st Army, directed that outstanding indents for the D.A.C. + Div. Train were to be sent to D.O. 1st Army Groups. Car sent to 1st Army Workshop for repairs.	Initials.

WAR DIARY / INTELLIGENCE SUMMARY

Army Form C. 2118

Place	Date	Hour	Summary of Events and Information	Remarks and references to Appendices
LA LACQUE	8.1.16		Outstanding indents for Div. Supply Column sent to C.O., Havre, and those of the Div. Am. Col. and Divnl. Train to the D.D. I.D.C. Army Troops. Paid in to Field Cashier, 11th Corps, the balance of Imprest a/c – 275 francs.	
LA LACQUE	9.1.16 10c/		Refs Remounts station by rail with Divnl. Hol. Res. for Marseilles.	wind
	10.1.16		On rail	
MARSEILLES	11.1.16		Arrived about 5 p.m. and proceeded to the Ordnance stores. On 4. was informed that very large demands for clothing &c. had been put forward by all units of the 46th Division. This is quite inexplicable, having in view the enormous quantities of clothing drawn by the Division previous to quitting the 11th Corps, and as a large quantity of 4.5" H.E. shell & Cart. for	
	12.1.16		shipment with Division.	wind

Army Form C. 2118

WAR DIARY
or
INTELLIGENCE SUMMARY
(Erase heading not required.)

84/

Instructions regarding War Diaries and Intelligence Summaries are contained in F. S. Regs., Part II. and the Staff Manual respectively. Title Pages will be prepared in manuscript.

Place	Date	Hour	Summary of Events and Information	Remarks and references to Appendices
MARSEILLES	13.1.16		Rde. Major. R.G.A. reported many draught hooks broken, to arrange with him to inspect all damages.	
	14.1.16		Visited all batteries with Rde. Major to ascertain damages to carriages. Gave instructions for local purchase in each case. The damages were principally broken draught hooks.	
	15.1.16		Received instructions from Ordnance, Communications that Khaki paint should be used for painting guns and artillery vehicles	wire.
	16.1.16		Arranged with D. A. D. O. S. to ship smoke helmets and ammunition on the S.S. "Bloemfontein Castledale"; Lieut. Corpl. Pierson + Pte. Young will accompany the consignment to destination. Brought two or three incidents to notice of Brit. Mil. Rep. for action, as they were, apparently, excessive.	wire.

1875 Wt. W593/826 1,000,000 4/15 J.B.C. & A. A.D.S.S./Forms/C. 2118.

Army Form C. 2118

WAR DIARY
or
INTELLIGENCE SUMMARY
(Erase heading not required.)

85

Instructions regarding War Diaries and Intelligence Summaries are contained in F.S. Regs., Part II. and the Staff Manual respectively. Title Pages will be prepared in manuscript.

Place	Date	Hour	Summary of Events and Information	Remarks and references to Appendices
MARSEILLES	17.1.16		All ammunition shipped on S.S. "Clan McCorquodale". O.C. complained about the want of clips for trimming horses, so agreed to local purchase of 4 for swingletrees.	nil
	18.1.16		Visited R.B.A. Brigade Hd. Bn. and gave instructions for repairs to wheel of a limber cart in possession of the 4th How. How.itzer Bde. The batteries of this Brigade were wanting large numbers of road nails & rivets with their limbers, so gave instructions that suitable chains should be purchased, if available.	nil
	19.1.16		Very little doing.	
	20.1.16		Received instructions from A.A. & Q.M.G. to embark on S.S. "Andania" tomorrow the 21 inst.	1
	21.1.16		Embarked on S.S. "Andania" at 10 am.	nil
	22.1.16		Received orders to disembark. Disembarked from S.S. "Andania".	nil

WAR DIARY
INTELLIGENCE SUMMARY
(Erase heading not required.)

Army Form C. 2118

Place	Date	Hour	Summary of Events and Information	Remarks and references to Appendices
MARSEILLES.	22.1.16		Indents from 1/1 N. M. Field Ambulance are received in rather insufficient notice of arriving 46' Division.	units.
	23.1.16		Very little doing	units.
	24.1.16		- do -	
	25.1.16		Entrained for Pont Remy.	units.
	26/1/16		-	
	27/1/16		Arrived at Pont Remy.	
PONT REMY.	28/1		Settled office & store in a Cinema Hall in the Rue Beaule'. A.D.o.S. 1st Army, visited office & Store. Directed that all unserviceable stores were to be returned to me by units.	units.
	29.1.16		Reported to C.D.o.S. 14 Corps. Received instructions from A.D.o.S. to demand Lewis guns, and additional transport allowed for Machine gun companies. Several Divisional orders (1087, 9, 90) issued, with a view to further economy in expenditure of clothing, &c., by units.	units.

Army Form C. 2118

WAR DIARY
or
INTELLIGENCE SUMMARY
(Erase heading not required.)

87

Instructions regarding War Diaries and Intelligence Summaries are contained in F. S. Regs., Part II. and the Staff Manual respectively. Title Pages will be prepared in manuscript.

Place	Date	Hour	Summary of Events and Information	Remarks and references to Appendices
PONT REMY	30.1.16		Called on O.D.O. 14' Corps. Also visited 14' Corps Ordnance Workshops. Drew 1,000 frames from Cardin, 14' Corps. Office connected up to Divnl. Telephone Exchange. This is more convenient.	urgs.
	31.1.16		Purchased timber in Abbeville for manufacture of bench for armourers shop. Also lamps for Divnl. Hd. Qr. Offices. Paint was received for painting vehicles with R.F.A. Groonin Cartain were instructed to purchase chains for use in lieu of brand ropes, the expansion of the latter article being enormous.	urgs. Winslades Major Bearer. L.C. Divn.

1875 Wt. W593/826 1,000,000 4/15 I.D.C. & A. A.D.S.S./Forms/C. 2118.

War Diary
of
Major W.W. Blades.
D.A.D.O.S. 46' Division.
From 1st. February. 1916.
to 29th. February. 1916.
Vol XII
W.W. Blades. Major.
D.A.D.O.S. 46' Division.

WAR DIARY
INTELLIGENCE SUMMARY

Army Form C. 2118

88

Place	Date	Hour	Summary of Events and Information	Remarks and references to Appendices
PONT REMY	1.2.16		Went to Abbeville, paid bill for timber, purchased 40 small donkey brushes. Went also to Picquigny to ascertain rates for various kinds of canvas. Prices for this material appear to be much higher than in the Amiens district. The first lot of harness was returned today by L. Staffs. Bn. R.O.A. the saddles required, at the moment, two new fleaps to make it S. Some breechings were in excellent condition. Brought the matter to notice of Divnl. Artillery H.Q., and Staff Captain came down to inspect the stores. This officer promised to send a representative from the Battery, to explain. It is obvious that judging by this first transaction, the return of unserviceable stores to bases, the reserve will be a large running to the hire.	corps

WAR DIARY
INTELLIGENCE SUMMARY

(Erase heading not required.)

Army Form C. 2118

Place	Date	Hour	Summary of Events and Information	Remarks and references to Appendices
PONT REMY	2.2.16		A number of Steel Helmets, catapults, bombs, throwers, sprayers, and 52 Lewis Guns were received from Base today. As much as possible was issued to 139th Infantry Brigade by Lorry. Endeavoured to find a firm in Abbeville to make breech covers, but failed.	xxvi.
	3.2.16		400 Dragees, 14,000 smoke helmets and 11 bicycles received from the Base. Made further endeavour to find a firm making breech covers but failed. Unserviceable clothing received from 5' Notts & Derby Regt. was duly examined, and enough to make a notice of a. a. + Q. m. g. many articles were considered fit for further wear. a. a. + Q. m. g. directed the articles to be returned to the unit.	xxvii.
	4.2.16		Went to Amiens to inquire for firm likely to make breech covers. Ordered 2000 from Mr Macquet, Rue des Sergents, Amiens for delivery on Monday, at a rate not to exceed 50 centimes each.	xxviii.

Army Form C. 2118

WAR DIARY
INTELLIGENCE SUMMARY

(Erase heading not required.)

Instructions regarding War Diaries and Intelligence Summaries are contained in F.S. Regs., Part II. and the Staff Manual respectively. Title Pages will be prepared in manuscript.

No. 90

Place	Date	Hour	Summary of Events and Information	Remarks and references to Appendices
PONT REMY	5.2.16		Visited Ordnance Depôt, Abbeville, with a view to getting names of contractors in the town, but was quite unsuccessful. The bulk of the tools for workshops arrived, and application was made to various locations for the personnel.	
	6.2.16		Very little doing today. Few units came to draw stores.	wwm
	7.2.16		Went to Quornfloi to see Bde Major 139th. Infantry Brigade, nothing important interesting.	wwm
	8.2.16		Morning fully occupied attending to enquirers. The first lot of boots for repair came in from Monmouth Regt. Details. Went to 14 Corps for three optical sights for trial in this Division.	wwm
	9.2.16		Went to Abbeville. Purchased a singer sewing machine for use in Workshop. also a few other small stores required. Took delivery of 1875 rifle pull covers from M. Prequet. Amiens. Also came in this evening that a long discussion on how was on the part of the unit.	wwm

WAR DIARY
INTELLIGENCE SUMMARY
(Erase heading not required.)

Army Form C. 2118

Place	Date	Hour	Summary of Events and Information	Remarks and references to Appendices
PONT REMY	10.2.16		Went to Abbeville to purchase forms, knives & nails. Car sent to Supply Column for overhaul. Received instructions from A.A. & Q.M.G. to demand five machine guns for the Stafford Infantry Bde. to replace others requiring overhaul. A number of horse shoes returned by 4i Scoff. Battery, R.F.A. & many found quite fit for a lot more wear, matter reported to A.D.V.S. This further proves the necessity for more leather received by units, the advantages of having all stores returned to O.R.D.	
	11.2.16		Received instructions from A.A. & Q.M.G. to provide camp equipment & change of underclothing for 1/4 Punish Regt. which is being isolated at Ailly. 75 Serge flatters arrived by lorry convoy & were sent on to Ailly. Further instructions received later to similarly provide for the 1/5 Punish Regt. & Monmouth Regts. C.O. came over to discuss the question & promised to send the additional tentage required as soon as he could get it from the base at Rouen. 1500 sets of underclothing & 3600 blankets were	

1875 Wt. W593/826 1,000,000 4/15 T.R.C.&A. A.D.S.S./Forms/C. 2118.

WAR DIARY / INTELLIGENCE SUMMARY

Army Form C. 2118

92

(Erase heading not required.)

Instructions regarding War Diaries and Intelligence Summaries are contained in F.S. Regs., Part II. and the Staff Manual respectively. Title Pages will be prepared in manuscript.

Place	Date	Hour	Summary of Events and Information	Remarks and references to Appendices
PONTREMY	11.2.16		Were also promised, on much an porcieres to be sent to Oilly this evening.	w.w.s.
	12.2.16		Went to Oilly, the Adv. H.Q. 138. Inf. Bde. Also to Bonneville to select new billets for detacht. when moving.	w.w.s.
	13.2.16		Went to new inits a view to securing satisfactory places for stores and workshops. Found such at Bonneville. Unserviceable clothing returned by 2nd. Lincoln Ratery, several jackets shorts were found serviceable, the only defect being that they were very dirty. This was enough to notice of A.A. + Q.M.G. who decided to see the articles tomorrow. Hd. Qrs. + part of 137th. Bde. arrived.	w.w.s.
	14.2.16		Reported at Hd. Qrs. of 137 Inf. Bde. and discussed equipment matters with the Brigadier. We did not desire to draw the Lewis guns for a day or so. St. Gratuelle reported for duty.	w.w.s.
	15.2.16		Visited Monmouth Regt. & 1/4 Lincoln Regt. Inadequate vehicles of former battalion required some minor repairs which I asked the O.C. to have carried out by the several artificers. Transport of the 1/4 Lincoln Regt. was in a good condition, so	w.w.s.

1875 Wt. W593/826 1,000,000 4/15 T.R.C. & A. A.D.S.S./Forms/C.2118.

Army Form C. 2118

Instructions regarding War Diaries and Intelligence Summaries are contained in F. S. Regs., Part II. and the Staff Manual respectively. Title Pages will be prepared in manuscript.

WAR DIARY or INTELLIGENCE SUMMARY

(Erase heading not required.)

Place	Date	Hour	Summary of Events and Information	Remarks and references to Appendices
PONT REMY	15.2.16		Was informed by the O.C. Practically all the vehicles of the Mounted Regt. required the existing machine fitted to wheels, the latter leaving far too much side play.	wu.m.
	16.2.16		Went to Abbeville & arranged with C.O.O. to send lorries for consignees of tents & clothing from 138th. Infantry Bde. to Abbeville. Visited 134th Infantry Bde. transport transport co company with Staff Captain, made arrangements that certain vehicles should be sent to 2.Coy. 17. Corps. Ordnance Workshops.	
	17.2.16		Q.O.1 came to store to inquire about stores for School of Instruction. He was told that all available stores were issued he could draw tomorrow. Arranged with Staff Captain 139th Inf. Bde. that stores for S.B. H.D. should be lorried out every 3 or 4 days.	wu.m.
	18.2.16		Went to 139th Inf. Bde. H.d. Rn. to investigate complaint of 6 hats. Early Regt. that ratchels for smoke helmets had been due to the unit since 29/12/15. Found that these were actually issued on 3.1.16. Complaint was also made that Pockets for smoke helmets were also required. These articles are due to arrive on Monday next an	wu.m. wu.m.

Army Form C. 2118

WAR DIARY
or
INTELLIGENCE SUMMARY
(Erase heading not required.)

Instructions regarding War Diaries and Intelligence Summaries are contained in F. S. Regs., Part II. and the Staff Manual respectively. Title Pages will be prepared in manuscript.

9 H /

Place	Date	Hour	Summary of Events and Information	Remarks and references to Appendices
PONT REMY	18.2.16		On leave. A lorry load of stores was sent to the School of Instruction at Peaweil.	wupt.
	19.2.16		Lorry sent to Peaweil with stores for School of Instruction, as promised. Went to Ribeaucourt to see keepers of stores coming in, and found all satisfactory. O.C. Reidhead wired that all truck had to be received, else they would be recornged. Replied that all available lorries were working and nothing more could be done. Moreover, the woollen clothing was urgently required for the 137th Infantry. Role first returned from a warm dinner.	
RIBEAUCOURT	20.2.16		Completed move to RIBEAUCOURT, O.C. 2nd Main claimed my office billet here, as it was taken with the knowledge of Camp Commandant. I told him I did not propose to turn out. Went to 2nd Army Head Quarters, near B.R.of. The large consumption of horses by 137th Inf. Bde was discussed.	wupt.

1875 Wt. W593/826 1,000,000 4/15 J.B.C. & A. A.D.S.S./Forms/C. 2118.

Army Form C. 2118

WAR DIARY
INTELLIGENCE SUMMARY
(Erase heading not required.)

95

Place	Date	Hour	Summary of Events and Information	Remarks and references to Appendices
RIBEAUCOURT	21.2.16		Went to Divisional School of Instruction at Beauval & discussed with the Adjutant the question of his equipment. Arranged to purchase what was required. Large consignment of winter clothing sent to the 134th Inf. Bde, also the Hammouth Regt. Two men were sent to hospital, one with rheumatics, the other hurt by a breakdown falling on his leg.	wen
	22.2.16		Went to Divl. School of Instruction at Beauval & saw the Comdt. Purchased Stoves & Ranges in Amiens & asked the School to send for them.	wen
	23.2.16		Cars sent to Column for overhaul, so had a day in, watching mechanics to units inspecting unserviceable stores returned. As few units returned stores, the following cases much make it quite clear that a most amount of preventative work must be taking place. Ro Lachets fit for further service were received from Contens repairs. They only required minor repairs & cleaning. One unit only required different sorts required glass only.	wen

1875 Wt. W593/826 1,000,000 4/15 J.B.C. & A. A.D.S.(S./Forms)/C. 2118.

Army Form C. 2118

WAR DIARY
or
INTELLIGENCE SUMMARY
(Erase heading not required.)

96

Place	Date	Hour	Summary of Events and Information	Remarks and references to Appendices
RIBEAUCOURT	23.2.16		only, to make them serviceable. Boots worn from new to a finish without being repaired. Shirts certified to be unserviceable merely because they required washing. It is also a waste even on the same scale in other Divisions the result must be appalling.	wzw/s
	24.2.16		Went to Achiere to inspect probable new billets for Div. Ho House, office, &c. seemed very good & accommodation sufficient. Went on to Amiens to purchase some camies for Divl. School of Instruction. Clothing received from G.S. Staff. Regt. on unserviceable this morning, was returned to the unit, on the built of it required minor repairs & cleaning only.	wzw/s
	25.2.16		Went to H6 Divl. School of Instruction with stores. Saw Comdt. Shoup front of mine units have lost their front cap, tape trenches, was fortunate enough to get two hundred weight of front nails.	wzw/s

1875 Wt. W593/826 1,000,000 4/15 J.B.C. & A. A.D.S.S./Forms/C. 2118.

Army Form C. 2118

Instructions regarding War Diaries and Intelligence Summaries are contained in F.S. Regs., Part II. and the Staff Manual respectively. Title Pages will be prepared in manuscript.

WAR DIARY
or
INTELLIGENCE SUMMARY
(Erase heading not required.)

9/

Place	Date	Hour	Summary of Events and Information	Remarks and references to Appendices
RIBEAUCOURT	26/2/16		Visited 137th Infantry Bde. Discussed the question of returns of unserviceable clothing	copy
	27.2.16		Received instructions from Gen. Staff to collect & hold for the present, all French thigh boots in the 137' Inf. Bde. Sent store by lorry to 3' Army School.	copy
	28.2.16		Went to Divl. School of Instruction. Searched could not see either the Comdt. or Adjutant. On return found that A.D.V.S. 17' Corps. had been to the office. Horses were replaced by horses transport today, with the result that stores were late in arriving at the stores. Drew 1000 francs from the field Cashier, 17' Corps. Called on Lt. Col. Sheppard, A.D.V.S. 17' Corps. 134th Infantry Bde. began to return French thigh boots. A great amount of new clothing was received by units today. Inspected the 134th Inf. Bde.	copy

Army Form C. 2118

WAR DIARY
or
INTELLIGENCE SUMMARY

(Erase heading not required.)

Instructions regarding War Diaries and Intelligence Summaries are contained in F. S. Regs., Part II. and the Staff Manual respectively. Title Pages will be prepared in manuscript.

No. 98

Place	Date	Hour	Summary of Events and Information	Remarks and references to Appendices
RIBEAUCOURT.	29.2.16		Received instructions from A.A.& Q.M.G. to leave this place tomorrow. Trench boots, reserve smoke helmets, & removal sprayers were loaded at Candas to be sent on to new railhead. But quite too many stores to move as on the last occasion. It is becoming clearer every day that the return of unserviceable stores tends to a far greater economy in quantities demanded to replace.	urgh.
				Wunloades Major S.A.D.O.S. 46 Division

29.2.16

D.A.D.O.S.
46th (N.M.) DIVISION Army Form C. 2118

AUGUST

Vol 15

WAR DIARY
INTELLIGENCE SUMMARY
(Erase heading not required.)

Place	Date	Hour	Summary of Events and Information	Remarks and references to Appendices
In the field	8/16 1		Handed over 72 Lewis Gun Magazines to O.O. VII Corps. Routine.	
"	2		Received instructions from Army to replace all Lewis guns with Vickers; also that in future all bulk indents for hard shoes are to be despatched so as to reach Calais on Sundays; also to send 7 Grenadier Brigadiers with special Grenadiers to Artillery. Settled weekly return of indents for tools, pickhelve, helmets etc.; also monthly return of bulk issues and of boots repaired in Divisional and Regimental shops.	
"	3		Settled weekly return of local purchases. Received memo from Havre that Division each mot to be equipped with short rifles under present circumstances and that all indents for same are cancelled.	
"	4 5 6 7		Routine. 24 Vickers guns arrived from base and distributed.	
"	8		Accident in Armourers shop; Private Tyler taken to Field Ambulance suffering from gun shot wound. Routine.	

Army Form C. 2118

WAR DIARY
INTELLIGENCE SUMMARY
(Erase heading not required.)

Instructions regarding War Diaries and Intelligence Summaries are contained in F. S. Regs., Part II. and the Staff Manual respectively. Title Pages will be prepared in manuscript.

Place	Date	Hour	Summary of Events and Information	Remarks and references to Appendices
In the field	8/16 9		Routine – including usual morning and evening visit to Div. H.Q.	
	10		Visited by Army Q.O.O. It informed me for reserve of instruction as D.A.D.O.S. Settled weekly return of breakages.	
	11.		Settled monthly return of brokerage in possession. Routine.	
	12		Enquiry as to cause of accident in armourer's shop on 7th inst. Finding that by mistake a live cartridge had got among the dummy cartridges in use in shop; shot in testing lewis gun bullet had inflicted a flesh wound after piercing armoury hall. Settled fortnightly cable & telephone return. Settled distribution of 70 British harmer sprayers among Divisional units.	
	13		Visited Corps D.Q. and looked over some musical instruments for the 7 46th Division. Routine.	
	14		Received instructions from A.D.O.S. that all dummy cartridges must have 8 holes bored through them to prevent confusion with live ones. Routine.	
	15.		Attended conference of Corps A.D.O.S's and other D.A.D.O.S's at Corps H.Q.	

WAR DIARY or INTELLIGENCE SUMMARY

Army Form C. 2118

Place	Date	Hour	Summary of Events and Information	Remarks and references to Appendices
In the field	8/16		Settled weekly anti-gas supplies. Steel helmets etc returned. S.M. Pearson sent to base and Sgt. Senard arrived to take over duties as O.O. of 137 Bde. Calais objected to Lewis gun parts being wired for	
	16			
	17		in exchange on account of length of wire. Anti aircraft batteries handed over for administration to O.O. Corps Troops. Settled local purchase return. Submitted plans prepared by Arm. S. Sgt. Cox to straightening Lewis gun to A.O.O.S.	
	18		Received Provisional Table for equipment of 9.45 trench mortar Batteries from A.O.O.S. Routine.	
	19		Received and distributed 750 Steel helmets.	
	20		} Routine.	
	21			
	22		Received and distributed 385 body shields for bombers in raids etc.	
	23		Received instructions from A.O.O.S. to issue Webb equipment to 147 A.T. bay, R.E. notwithstanding A.R.O. of 29 May. Issued further 850 Steel helmets. Settled weekly return of audit for helmets etc.	
	24		Settled weekly return of local purchases. Routine.	
	25		Routine	

Army Form C. 2118

WAR DIARY
or
INTELLIGENCE SUMMARY
(Erase heading not required.)

Instructions regarding War Diaries and Intelligence Summaries are contained in F. S. Regs., Part II. and the Staff Manual respectively. Title Pages will be prepared in manuscript.

Place	Date	Hour	Summary of Events and Information	Remarks and references to Appendices
In the field	8/16 26 27 28		Routine. Settled Cable & Telephone Return and Nor. of A.O.D. and A.O.C, also Return of average number of permanent labourers employed daily.	
	29 30 31		Visited D.O.s of 137th and 139th Brigades. Idents checked by growth hasten of units and certificate to that effect sent the Corps D.R.	

M Macnab Capt
B.P.D.V.S. 46th Div.

1875 Wt. W593/826 1,000,000 4/15 T.R.C. & A. A.D.S.S./Forms/C. 2118.

Herewith War Diary of D.A.D.O.S. 46th Division for September, October & both Diaries of September & October in response to your call yos/same date 2/11/16.

Army Form C. 2118

DADOS 46th Div
Vol 19 - 20
& 21

WAR DIARY
or
INTELLIGENCE SUMMARY
(Erase heading not required.)

Instructions regarding War Diaries and Intelligence Summaries are contained in F. S. Regs., Part II. and the Staff Manual respectively. Title Pages will be prepared in manuscript.

Place	Date	Hour	Summary of Events and Information	Remarks and references to Appendices
DAVIGNCOURT	September 1st.		Routine.	
	2nd.		Visited 137th. Bde. H.Q. re Machine Guns.	
	3rd.		Routine.	
	4th.		"	
	5th.		Visited I.O.M. re repair of Vehicles.	
	6th.		Routine.	
	7th.		D.DWO.S. 3rd. Army came. Went to conference A.D.O.S. VII Corps.	
	8th.		A.D.O.S. Went round Stores.	
	9th.		Routine.	
	10th.		"	
	11th.		Visited 138th. Bde. H.Q.	
	12th.		Carried out experiments with Lewis Henderson G.O.C. & A.A. & Q.M.G. present.	
	13th.		Routine. Fire's lot of M.G. Helmets received.	
	14th.		Lewis Gun officers came to see kits of handcarts.	
	15th.		Bought Stores at Doullens for 139th. Bde. A.D.O.S. called.	
	16th.		First Helmets received. (3000).	

1875 Wt. W593/826 1,000,000 4/15 T.R.C. & A. A.D.S.S./Forms/C. 2118.

Army Form C. 2118

M501 46 Div

WAR DIARY
or
INTELLIGENCE SUMMARY
(Erase heading not required.)

Instructions regarding War Diaries and Intelligence Summaries are contained in F.S. Regs., Part II. and the Staff Manual respectively. Title Pages will be prepared in manuscript.

Place	Date	Hour	Summary of Events and Information	Remarks and references to Appendices
	December			
	17th.		Routine. Visited 138th Bde H.Q.	
	18th.		Routine.	
	19th.		Lieut McGorm left for Salonica. 4p.m.	
	20th.		Routine.	
	21st.		Visited all Bde H.Q.	
	22nd.		Routine.	
	23rd.		"	
	24th.		"	
	25th.		"	
	26th.		Visited Field Amb & Dumps and found satisfactory.	
	27th.		Routine.	
	28th.		"	
	29th.		"	
	30th.		"	

Lawrence Capt
D.D.M.S. 46 Div

Army Form C. 2118

WAR DIARY
or
INTELLIGENCE SUMMARY
(Erase heading not required.)

Instructions regarding War Diaries and Intelligence Summaries are contained in F. S. Regs., Part II. and the Staff Manual respectively. Title Pages will be prepared in manuscript.

Place	Date	Hour	Summary of Events and Information	Remarks and references to Appendices
BALLOGNE.	Oct'ber.			
	1st.		Routine.	
	2nd.		"	
	3rd.		"	
	4th.		Major Legros. D.A.D.M.S. visited store & shops to-day.	
	5th.		Routine.	
	6th.		"	
	7th.		"	
	8th.		"	
	9th.		"	
	10th.		Staff S'gt M. R.A. sent to hospital Mechanism for A.M.S.	
	11th.		Routine.	
	12th.		Left for leave to England for 10 days.	
	13th.			
	14th.			
	15th.			
	16th.			
	17th.		Leave.	
	18th.			
	19th.			
	20th.			
	21st.			
	22nd.			
	23rd.		Routine.	
	24th.		"	
	25th.		"	
	26th.		"	
	27th.		"	
	28th.		"	
	29th.		Started packing up for move. No stores issued.	
	30th.		Held Inspection & sent all stores to Rouen-le-Grand.	
	31st.		S/Condr O'Neil left for duty with 3rd. Army.	

Army Form C. 2118

WAR DIARY
or
INTELLIGENCE SUMMARY
(Erase heading not required.)

DADS /6 Bn

Instructions regarding War Diaries and Intelligence Summaries are contained in F.S. Regs., Part II. and the Staff Manual respectively. Title Pages will be prepared in manuscript.

Place	Date	Hour	Summary of Events and Information	Remarks and references to Appendices

Army Form C. 2118

S.A.D.O.S.

WAR DIARY
or
INTELLIGENCE SUMMARY
(Erase heading not required.)

46th Division

1st 27th December 1916

J.M. Maxwell Captain
D.A.D.O.S
46th Division

Army Form C. 2118

WAR DIARY
or
INTELLIGENCE SUMMARY

(Erase heading not required.)

COPY

D.A.D.O.S. 4th Div.

For January 1917

Vol 19

Instructions regarding War Diaries and Intelligence Summaries are contained in F. S. Regs., Part II. and the Staff Manual respectively. Title Pages will be prepared in manuscript.

Place	Date	Hour	Summary of Events and Information	Remarks and references to Appendices
HENU	January 1		⎫	
	2		⎪	
	3		⎪	
	4		⎬ ROUTINE	
	5		⎪	
	6		⎪	
	7		⎪	
	8		⎭	
	9		⎫	
	10		⎪	
	11		⎪	
	12		⎪	
	13		⎬ ON LEAVE	
	14		⎪	
	15		⎪	
	16		⎪	
	17		⎭	
	18		⎫	
	19		⎪	
	20		⎪	
	21		⎪	
	22		⎪	
	23		⎪	
	24		⎬ ROUTINE	
	25		⎪	
	26		⎪	
	27		⎪	
	28		⎪	
	29		⎪	
	30		⎪	
	31		⎭	

1875 Wt. W593/826 1,000,000 4/15 J.B.C. & A. A.D.S.S./Forms/C. 2118.

D.A.D.O.S - 46th DIVISION   FEBRUARY.   Vol 24

Army Form C. 2118

WAR DIARY
or
INTELLIGENCE SUMMARY
(Erase heading not required.)

Instructions regarding War Diaries and Intelligence Summaries are contained in F. S. Regs., Part II. and the Staff Manual respectively. Title Pages will be prepared in manuscript.

Place	Date	Hour	Summary of Events and Information	Remarks and references to Appendices
HENU.	February			
	1			
	2			
	3			
	4			
	5		Routine	
	6			
	7			
	8			
	9			
	10			
	11			
	12			
	13			
	14			
	15			
	16			
	17			
	18			
	19			
	20		D.H.Q. moved to GOUY. Stores & office remain at HENU.	
	21			
	22			
	23			
	24		Routine, went to GOUY every day to D.H.Q.	
	25			
	26			
	27			
	28			

Army Form C. 2118

WAR DIARY
or
INTELLIGENCE SUMMARY
(Erase heading not required.)

Instructions regarding War Diaries and Intelligence Summaries are contained in F. S. Regs., Part II. and the Staff Manual respectively. Title Pages will be prepared in manuscript.

SADOS
for March 1917.
Vol 21
46 Division

Place	Date	Hour	Summary of Events and Information	Remarks and references to Appendices
	MARCH			
	1		Routine	
	2			
	3			
	4			
	5		Transferred to 5 Corps, 5 Army	
	6			
	7			
HENU	8			
	9			
	10		Routine	
	11			
	12			
	13			
	14			
	15			
	16			
	17			
	18			
	19			
	20			
COUIN	21		Moved Stores etc to COUIN, no stores issued	
"	22		Opened stores etc. Units drew stores this day	
"	23		Routine	
VILLERS BOCAGE	24		Left COUIN moved to VILLERS BOCAGE	
"	25		No stores issued, lorries no unloaded	
DURY	26		Left VILLERS BOCAGE moved to DURY - LORRIES with stores left by road to FONTES	
IN CAR	27		left by car to new area to find suitable stores etc.	
VILLERS	28		PERSONNEL LEFT BY TRAIN for new area	
FONTES	29		found suitable place for stores	
"	30		Personnel arrived also two truck fulls of stores from old area	
"	31		Opened store, stores for issue	31/3/17

WAR DIARY
or
INTELLIGENCE SUMMARY

(Erase heading not required.)

Army Form C. 2118

DADOS 462

Apl 22

Instructions regarding War Diaries and Intelligence Summaries are contained in F. S. Regs., Part II. and the Staff Manual respectively. Title Pages will be prepared in manuscript.

Place	Date	Hour	Summary of Events and Information	Remarks and references to Appendices
FONTES	APRIL			
"	1			
"	2			
"	3			
"	4			
"	5			
"	6		Routine	
"	7			
"	8			
"	9			
"	10			
"	11			
"	12			
"	13		Left FONTES moved to BUSNES. Opened Store & office	
BUSNES	14		Routine.	
"	15			
"	16		Left BUSNES moved to LEBEUVRIERE. Hardly any Store issued, troops moving	
LEBEUVRIERE	17			
"	18			
"	19		Left LEBEUVRIERE moved to SAINS. Open store	
SAINS	20		Moved Store to another part of SAINS	
"	21			
"	22			
"	23		Routine.	
"	24			
"	25			
"	26			
"	27			
"	28			
"	29			
"	30			

D.A.D.O.S.
46th Division

30/4/17.

Army Form C. 2118

WAR DIARY
or
INTELLIGENCE SUMMARY
(Erase heading not required.)

DADS 462

Vol 23

Place	Date	Hour	Summary of Events and Information	Remarks and references to Appendices
SAINS-EN-GOHELLE	MAY 1–26		General Routine, nothing of importance to record.	
	27–31		On leave to England.	

M Maxwell Capt
DADS 46 Div

Army Form C. 2118

WAR DIARY
or
INTELLIGENCE SUMMARY
(Erase heading not required.)

DADS46D JR24

Place	Date	Hour	Summary of Events and Information	Remarks and references to Appendices
SAINS-EN-GOHELLE.	JUNE 1 2 3 4 5 6 7 8 9 10 11 12 13 14 15 16 17 18 19 20 21 22 23 24 25 26 27 28 29 30		Routine, nothing of importance to record. —	

J M Maxwell Capt.
DADS. 46th Division.

WAR DIARY or INTELLIGENCE SUMMARY

Army Form C. 2118

Vol 25

Place	Date	Hour	Summary of Events and Information	Remarks and references to Appendices
SAINS-EN-GOHELLE.	JULY 1		Packing up for move to rest area -	
	2		Left SAINS for OURTON	
	3		No store issued	
	4		Started issuing stores -	
	5			
	6			
	7			
	8			
	9			
	10			
	11			
	12			
	13			
OURTON.	14		General Routine	
	15			
	16			
	17			
	18			
	19			
	20			
	21			
	22			
	23			
	24			
	25		Left OURTON & arrived at LABOURSE	
	26		Opened issued Stores - LIEUT.CHAPLIN attached for instruction. -	
	27			
LABOURSE.	28		Routine. Dump very unsuitable for Ordnance.	
	29		Improved by building extra sheds & roads.	
	30			
	31			

1875 Wt. W593/826 1,000,000 4/15 T.R.C. & A. A.D.S.S./Forms/C. 2118.

Army Form C. 2118

WAR DIARY
or
INTELLIGENCE SUMMARY
(Erase heading not required.)

Vol 26

Instructions regarding War Diaries and Intelligence Summaries are contained in F. S. Regs., Part II. and the Staff Manual respectively. Title Pages will be prepared in manuscript.

Place	Date	Hour	Summary of Events and Information	Remarks and references to Appendices
	AUGUST			
LABOURSE	1 / 2 / 3 / 4 / 5 / 6 / 7 / 8 / 9 / 10 / 11 / 12 / 13 / 14 / 15 / 16 / 17 / 18 / 19 / 20 / 21 / 22 / 23 / 24 / 25 / 26 / 27 / 28 / 29 / 30 / 31.		General Routine, nothing Special to report. —	

J M Maxwell Capt
D.A.D.S.S. 46th Div

1875 Wt. W503/826 1,000,000 4/15 I.R.C. & A. A.D.S.S./Forms/C. 2118.

WAR DIARY
or
INTELLIGENCE SUMMARY

Army Form C. 2118

AD S 346

Vol 27

Place	Date	Hour	Summary of Events and Information	Remarks and references to Appendices
LABOUR S.E.	SEPTEMBER.			
	1			
	2			
	3		General Roulin –	
	4			
	5			
	6			
	7			
	8			
	9			
	10		Major-General Sir J. Stevens, KCB, Major-General Parsons CB. inspected Store Wksps with Colonel Forbes ADST Brit. Army	
	11			
	12			
	13			
	14			
	15			
	16			
	17			
	18		General Roulin –	
	19			
	20			
	21			
	22			
	23			
	24			
	25			
	26			
	27			
	28			
	29			
	30			

30/9/17.

Army Form C. 2118

WAR DIARY
or
INTELLIGENCE SUMMARY
(Erase heading not required.)

Place	Date	Hour	Summary of Events and Information	Remarks and references to Appendices
LABOURSE	OCTOBER			
	1			
	2			
	3			
	4			
	5			
	6			
	7			
	8			
	9			
	10			
	11			
	12			
	13		General Routine, nothing important to report.	
	14			
	15			
	16			
	17			
	18			
	19			
	20			
	21			
	22			
	23			
	24			
	25			
LABOURSE	26			
	27			
	28			
	29			
	30			
	31			

WAR DIARY
or
INTELLIGENCE SUMMARY
(Erase heading not required.)

Army Form C. 2118

Darts 469

Vol 29

November 13 - 30, 1917

Place	Date	Hour	Summary of Events and Information	Remarks and references to Appendices
LABOURSE			General Routine. Nothing important to report —	

M Maxwell Capt ADu
ADuS 46 Div

Army Form C. 2118

WAR DIARY
or
INTELLIGENCE SUMMARY
(Erase heading not required.)

DADS 287 — 67th Div Vol 30

Place	Date	Hour	Summary of Events and Information	Remarks and references to Appendices
LABOURSE	DECEMBER 1,2,3,4,5,6,7,8,9,10		ROUTINE	
	11		On leave to England. Lieut Lumie A.O.O. did duty as D.A.D.O.S.	
	12,13,14,15,16,17			
	18		Lieut Lumie left for 11th Division	
	19		Started to move Stores etc to BUSNES	
	20		Moved to BUSNES	
	21		Started issuing Stores from dump at BUSNES	
	22,23,24,25,26			
BUSNES	27,28,29,30,31		General Routine.	

Instructions regarding War Diaries and Intelligence Summaries are contained in F.S. Regs., Part II. and the Staff Manual respectively. Title Pages will be prepared in manuscript.

Army Form C. 2118

WAR DIARY
or
INTELLIGENCE SUMMARY
(Erase heading not required.)

Instructions regarding War Diaries and Intelligence Summaries are contained in F. S. Regs., Part II. and the Staff Manual respectively. Title Pages will be prepared in manuscript.

Place	Date	Hour	Summary of Events and Information	Remarks and references to Appendices
	JANUARY 1916			
LABOURSE	1			
	2			
	3			
	4			
	5			
	6		Routine	
	7			
	8			
	9			
	10			
	11			
	12			
	13			
	14			
	15			
	16			
	17		Started moving stores to new area, BUSNES-	
	18		head mess tents & personnel to BUSNES	
	19		considered over.	
BUSNES	20			
	21			
	22			
	23			
	24		Routine	
	25			
	26			
	27			
	28			
	29			
	30			
	31			

Army Form C. 2118

WAR DIARY
or
INTELLIGENCE SUMMARY
(Erase heading not required.)

Instructions regarding War Diaries and Intelligence Summaries are contained in F. S. Regs., Part II. and the Staff Manual respectively. Title Pages will be prepared in manuscript.

Place	Date	Hour	Summary of Events and Information	Remarks and references to Appendices
	FEBRUARY			
BUSNES.	1		Routine	
	2			
	3			
	4			
	5		Started moving to BOMY	
	6		Stores rations opened at BOMY	
	7			
BOMY	8			
	9			
	10			
	11			
	12			
	13			
	14			
	15		General Routine	
	16			
	17			
	18			
	19			
	20			
	21			
	22			
	23			
	24			
	25			
	26			
	27			
	28			

WAR DIARY
INTELLIGENCE SUMMARY
(Erase heading not required.)

Army Form C. 2118

DADS 767
Vol 33

Place	Date	Hour	Summary of Events and Information	Remarks and references to Appendices
BOMY	MARCH 1		Routine	
	2			
FOUQUIERES	3			
	4			
	5			
	6			
	7		Acted as A.D.O.S. I Corps.	
	8			
	9			
	10			
	11			
	12			
	13			
	14		Lt. H.S CLAPHAM arrived for duty	
	15			
	16			
	17			
	18		Routine	
	19			
	20			
	21			
	22			
	23			
	24			
	25			
	26			
	27			
	28			
BRACQUEMONT	29		Moved to BRACQUEMONT	
	30		General Routine	
	31			

WAR DIARY
or
INTELLIGENCE SUMMARY

Army Form C. 2118

DADS 462
WO 95/34

Place	Date	Hour	Summary of Events and Information	Remarks and references to Appendices
BRACQUEMONT	APRIL 1			
	2			
	3			
	4			
	5		Routine. —	
	6			
do	7			
	8			
	9			
	10			
	11			
	12		Left BRACQUEMONT to BRUAY	
BRUAY	13			
	14			
	15		Routine	
	16			
	17			
	18			
	19		Capt. A. NIXON. A.O.D. arrived for instruction. —	
do	20			
	21		Routine.	
	22			
	23			
	24		Moved from BRUAY to GOSNAY.	
GOSNAY.	25			
	26			
do	27		Routine. —	
	28			
	29			
	30			

J. Maxwell. Capt.
ADDS ubMti.

Army Form C. 2118.

WAR DIARY
or
INTELLIGENCE SUMMARY.

(Erase heading not required.)

Instructions regarding War Diaries and Intelligence Summaries are contained in F. S. Regs., Part II. and the Staff Manual respectively. Title pages will be prepared in manuscript.

Place	Date	Hour	Summary of Events and Information	Remarks and references to Appendices

Army Form C. 2118.

WAR DIARY
INTELLIGENCE SUMMARY.
(Erase heading not required.)

Instructions regarding War Diaries and Intelligence
Summaries are contained in F.S. Regs., Part II.
and the Staff Manual respectively. Title pages
will be prepared in manuscript.

Place	Date	Hour	Summary of Events and Information	Remarks and references to Appendices

Army Form C. 2118.

DADT 846D Vol 37

WAR DIARY
or
INTELLIGENCE SUMMARY.
(Erase heading not required.)

Place	Date	Hour	Summary of Events and Information	Remarks and references to Appendices
GOSNAY	July		General Routine	

WAR DIARY

INTELLIGENCE SUMMARY

Army Form C. 2118.

(Erase heading not required.)

Instructions regarding War Diaries and Intelligence Summaries are contained in F. S. Regs., Part II. and the Staff Manual respectively. Title pages will be prepared in manuscript.

Place	Date	Hour	Summary of Events and Information	Remarks and references to Appendices
GOSNAY.	Sept 1st.	1918.		
	" 2nd.	do		
	" 3rd.	do		
	" 4th.	do		
	" 5th.	do	Routine work.	
	" 6th.	do		
	" 7th.	do		
	" 8th.	do		
	" 9th.	do		
	" 10th.	do	Handed over Tents and area stores to XIII Corps.	
	" 11th.	do	Prepared for move.	
BEAUCOURT.	" 12th.	do	Moved to Beaucourt.	
	" 13th.	do		
	" 14th.	do		
	" 15th.	do	Routine work.	
	" 16th.	do		
	" 17th.	do		
	" 18th.	do	Surplus kit sent to Ribemont to be stored.	
	" 19th.	do	Moved to Tertry. No accommodation at Tertry- moved to Estree	
ESTREE.	" 20th.	do		
	" 21st.	do		
	" 22nd.	do		
	" 23rd.	do	Routine work.	
	" 24th.	do		
	" 25th.	do		
	" 26th.	do		

Army Form C. 2118.

WAR DIARY
INTELLIGENCE SUMMARY.
(Erase heading not required.)

Instructions regarding War Diaries and Intelligence Summaries are contained in F. S. Regs., Part II. and the Staff Manual respectively. Title pages will be prepared in manuscript.

Place	Date	Hour	Summary of Events and Information	Remarks and references to Appendices
Estrees	Sept 27th. 1918.		Lifebelts for Bellenglise attack received from Boulogne and issued.	
"	" 28th.	do		
"	" 29th.	do	Nothing to report. Routine.	
"	" 30th.	do		

Army Form C. 2118.

WAR DIARY
or
INTELLIGENCE SUMMARY.
(*Erase heading not required.*)

Instructions regarding War Diaries and Intelligence Summaries are contained in F. S. Regs., Part II. and the Staff Manual respectively. Title pages will be prepared in manuscript.

Place	Date October 1918.	Hour	Summary of Events and Information	Remarks and references to Appendices
ESTREES.	Oct.	1st		
"	"	2nd.		
"	"	3rd.		
"	"	4th.	Routine Work.	
"	"	5th.		
"	"	6th.		
"	"	7th.		
"	"	8th.		
VENDELLES.	"	9th.	Moved to Vendelles.	
"	"	10th.		
"	"	11th.		
"	"	12th.		
"	"	13th.	Routine work. Convoys sent out each day	
"	"	14th.	to Brigades with stores.	
"	"	15th.		
"	"	16th.		
"	"	17th.		
"	"	18th.		
SEQUEHART.	"	19th.	Moved to SEQUEHART.	
"	"	20th.		
"	"	21st.		
"	"	22nd.		
"	"	23rd.	Routine work.	
"	"	24th.		
"	"	25th.		
"	"	26th.	Leave to Paris.	
"	"	27th.	ROUTINE WORK.	
"	"	28th.	Moved to Fresnoy.	
FRESNOY.	"	29th.		
"	"	30th.	Routine work.	
"	"	31st.		

Army Form C. 2118.

WAR DIARY
or
INTELLIGENCE SUMMARY.
(Erase heading not required.)

Instructions regarding War Diaries and Intelligence Summaries are contained in F. S. Regs., Part II. and the Staff Manual respectively. Title pages will be prepared in manuscript.

Place	Date	Hour	Summary of Events and Information	Remarks and references to Appendices
	November 1918.			
FRESNOY.	1st.			
"	2nd.			
"	3rd.		Routine work.	
"	4th.			
"	5th.			
	6th.		Moved to Catillon.	
CATILLON.	7th.			
"	8th.		Routine.	
"	9th.			
"	10th.			
"	11th.			
"	12th.		Moved to Sam Sains du Nord.	
SAMS DU NORD.	13th.		Routine.	
"	14th.		Moved to Landrecies.	
LANDRECIES.	15th.			
"	16th.			
"	17th.			
"	18th.			
"	19th.			
"	20th.			
"	21st.		Nothing to report. Routine.	
"	22nd.			
"	23rd.			
"	24th.			
"	25th.			
"	26th.			
"	27th.			
"	28th.			
"	29th.			
"	30th.			

Army Form C. 2118.

WAR DIARY
or
INTELLIGENCE-SUMMARY.
(*Erase heading not required.*)

Instructions regarding War Diaries and Intelligence Summaries are contained in F. S. Regs., Part II. and the Staff Manual respectively. Title pages will be prepared in manuscript.

Place	Date	Hour	Summary of Events and Information	Remarks and references to Appendices
LANDRECIES.	December 1918.			
"	1st.			
"	2nd.			
"	3rd.			
"	4th.			
"	5th.			
"	6th.			
"	7th.			
"	8th.			
"	9th.		Routine Work.	
"	10th.			
"	11th.			
"	12th.			
"	13th.			
"	14th.			
"	15th.			
"	16th.			
"	17th.			
"	18th.		Arrival of Lt K.M.HEWSON. R.A.O.C.	
"	19th.		Attended Q.Ms. meeting.	
"	20th.		Visiting Units with COL. MANUELLE.	
"	21st.		Visited Railhead.	
"	22nd.		Routine.	
"	23rd.		Took over papers etc from Col. Manuelle.	
"	24th.		COL. MANUELLE departed to take up duties	
"	25th.		as A.D.O.S. XXII Corps.	
"	26th.		Routine.	
"	27th.		Visited BOHAIN to arrange billets.	
"	28th.		Routine Work.	
"	29th.			
"	30th.		Move to BOHAIN cancelled.	
"	31st.			

Army Form C. 2118.

WAR DIARY
or
INTELLIGENCE-SUMMARY.

(Erase heading not required.)

Place	Date	Hour	Summary of Events and Information	Remarks and references to Appendices
LANDRECIES	Jan. 1. 1919.		Routine.	
"	2.		Visited Busigny for arranging dump for demobilization	
"	3.		Routine.	
"	4.		Visited 139th Bde.	
"	5.		Visited Vaux Audigny to arrange removal of stores from 9th Corps Reception Camp.	
"	6.		Routine.	
"	7.		Demand sent to Base for Third blanket per man. Visited Railhead.	
"	8.		Routine.	
"	9.		Moved to Le Cateau.	
Le CATEAU.	10.		Routine.	
"	11.		Routine.	
"	12.		Delivering Stores to 137th and 139th Bde.	
"	13.		Removing 20 tons of salvage from La Groise. Third blanket received.	
"	14.		Visited 139th Infy Bde. Inspected remainder of salvage at La Groise.	
"	15.		Routine.	
"	16.		Lamps delivered to Area Commandants in Divisional Area.	
"	17.		Visited 13th Corps and inspected quantity of pontoon Stores at Grand Payt.	
"	18.		Routine.	
"	19.		Visited 139th Bde re Clothing and boots.	
"	20.		Visited Le Cateau Railhead.	
"	21.		Routine.	
"	22.		Visited 139th Bde and inspected workshops.	
"	23.		Visited 137th Bde.	
"	24.		Visited 138th Bde.	
"	25.		Routine.	
"	26.		Visited the Monmouth Regt.	
"	27.		Routine.	

ADOS, 46th Division

Army Form C. 2118.

WAR DIARY
or
INTELLIGENCE-SUMMARY.

(Erase heading not required.)

Place	Date	Hour	Summary of Events and Information	Remarks and references to Appendices
Le Cateau	Jan. 1919. 28.	-	Moved to different office in Le Cateau.	
"	29.	-	Routine.	
"	30.	-	Routine.	
"	31.	-	Routine.	

M————
Major
DADOS, 46th Division.

46th. Division.
No. W.D. 2.

D.A.G.,
  3rd Echelon,
    B A S E.
****

    Herewith War Diaries of D.A.D.O.S., 46th.
Division for month of February, 1919.

                        Brigadier-General,
               Commanding 46th. Division....

30th March, 1919.

Army Form C. 2118.

WAR DIARY
or
INTELLIGENCE SUMMARY.

(Erase heading not required.)

Instructions regarding War Diaries and Intelligence
Summaries are contained in F. S. Regs., Part II.
and the Staff Manual respectively. Title pages
will be prepared in manuscript.

Place	Date	Hour	Summary of Events and Information	Remarks and references to Appendices
Le Cateau.	1919. Feb.1st.		Routine.	
"	" 2.		"	
"	" 3.		"	
"	" 4.		Visited Ors to select site for Intermediate collecting Stn	
"	" 5.		Routine.	
"	" 6.		Routine.	
"	" 7.		Visited 139th Bde.	
"	" 8.		Routine.	
"	" 9.		Routine.	
"	" 10.		Visited XIII Corps to arrange re new site for I.C.S. near Caudry.	
"	" 11.		Visited 138 & 139 Bdes.	
"	" 12.		Visited Gun Park & R.A.	
"	" 13.		Routine.	
"	" 14.		Selecting lock up place at Caudry for storage for valuable stores on demobilization.	
"	" 15.		Acting A.D.O.S. XIII Corps.	
"	" 16.		do do do	
"	" 17.		do do	
"	" 18.		do do	
"	" 19.		do do	
"	" 20.		Routine.	
"	" 21.		Routine.	
"	" 22.		Routine.	
"	" 23.		Selecting site with D.A.Q.M.G. for vehicle park.	
"	" 24.		Routine.	
"	" 25.		Routine.	
"	" 26.		Routine.	
"	" 27.		Routine.	
"	" 28.		Routine.	

DADOS, 46th Division.

www.ingramcontent.com/pod-product-compliance
Lightning Source LLC
Chambersburg PA
CBHW081548160426
43191CB00011B/1866